Granny Needs My Help

A Child's Look at Dementia
and Alzheimer's

Written by
Deborah L Mills

WALKER LAYNE
GROUP

The information in this book is based on the author's experience. Some sample scenarios in this book are fictitious. This book does not replace the advice of a medical professional.

Granny Needs My Help: A Child's Look at Dementia and Alzheimer's

ISBN-978-1-7361800-1-3

walkerlaynegroup.com

Copyright©2020 Deborah L Mills

All rights reserved. No part of this book may be reproduced, stored in a retrieval system, transmitted in any form or by any means – electronic, mechanical, photocopying, recording, or otherwise – without prior permission in writing from the publisher.

Walker Layne Group, LLC

For bulk purchases, author interviews, local classroom visits and more contact the publisher.

A Special Note to
THE BIG KIDS

The pictures in this book are big and bright. Smaller kids like big, bright pictures. Many big kids do too. Smaller kids like to "read" the pictures. Because you are bigger, you can enjoy the big, bright pictures and even read this book all by yourself. If there is anything you don't understand, please ask a grownup.

Okay, let's get started.

My name is Zéh; it rhymes with "say," and I'm so happy to meet you.

I want to tell you about me and my granny and a new word I learned.

My granny is the best in the world.

She's beautiful, kind, and she does fun things. Things like dancing and snapping her fingers,

playing jack rocks as she calls it, and making funny faces.

We did tons of things together.
Granny helped me a lot.
She liked to take me by the hand when we crossed the street, to make sure I was safe from harm.

She held me tight every night and let me know everything was okay.
This is the way it was, and the way I thought it always would be, my granny helping to care for me.

But something changed, and things are really different. Instead of Granny holding my hand, I hold hers, and I help make sure she is alright.

"Granny needs our help, Zéh," Mommy explained. "There's something going on in Granny's brain.

Your brain tells you how to walk and speak.
It tells you when to stand or take a seat.
Your brain helps you think and remember.
Your brain reminds you August comes before September."

The plants we planted?

The dances we danced?"

Mommy said, "Instead of remembering and telling her what to do, Granny's brain is forgetting. She may forget me and you."

"She may forget how to make decisions, how to do simple tasks like take a bath and go to the bathroom.

She may get confused, scared, or angry, and not know what to do.

She may not understand that you are really you."

At first, I was a little **sad**,

a little **mad**,

even a little **afraid**.

But most of all, my heart was **broken**.

"How can this be! I don't understand."
So, Mommy explained it once again.

"The doctor says it is a form of dementia. It is called **Alzheimer's**.

It changes the brain and tries to take over like weeds in a garden."

I was sad to think of all the things Granny would forget. The weeds were trying to take over, but they hadn't yet.

Granny was forgetting, but I needed to REMEMBER.

REMEMBER the fun we already had and the fun we were going to have.

I thought of the time Granny and I played in the rain. We were soaking wet from head to toe.

It made me laugh and smile to know, Granny loves me all the same, whether or not she remembers my name.

It's okay to be sad, I told myself. But I can't stay sad. Granny needs my help.

With Mommy's permission,

I'll hold her hand when we go to the park.

I'll turn on the lights when it gets dark.

I may be small, but there is a lot I can do.

My granny needs me, and I'll come through.

Granny likes to whistle and play with dolls. She colors with crayons too.

Sometimes she colors on the table. What can you do?

Mommy doesn't get mad. I'm not ashamed when she makes a mess.

I just remember she's doing her very best.

I'm not afraid anymore, and I don't get sad or mad so much.

I just want Granny to remember.

"Zéh, my name is Zéh.
Please remember me!"

I get angry at dementia and want to throw it into the sea.

Staying mad wouldn't do any good. I'd just miss all the fun we still have to share.

So, I choose to be happy even when life isn't fair.

She's not like she was because of her brain, yet she's my granny just the same.

When I feel happy, sad, or mad I talk to my mom.

She understands dementia far better than me. She got me a journal where my thoughts can be free.

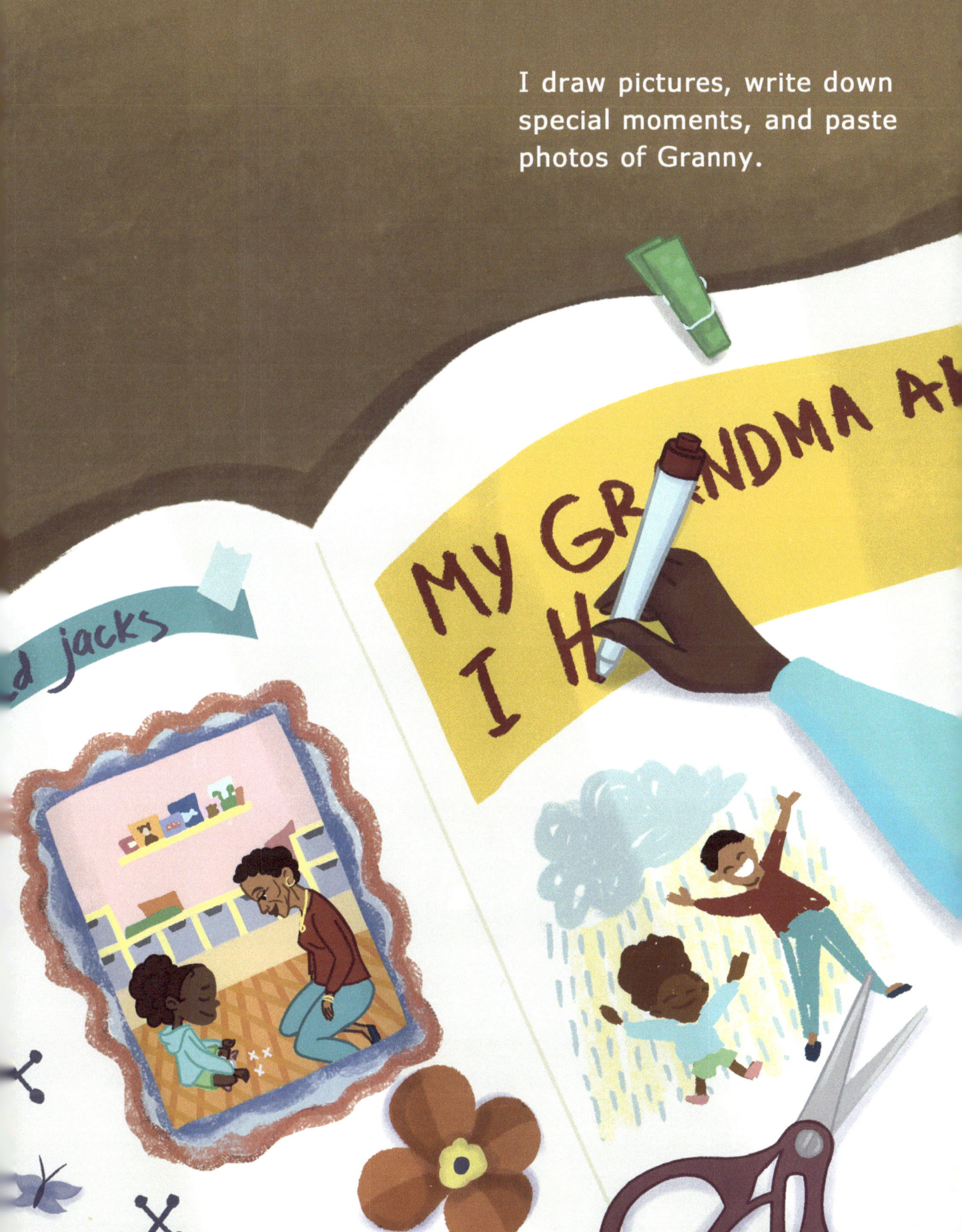

I draw pictures, write down special moments, and paste photos of Granny.

Dementia is the new word I've learned. It's a disease in the brain. It causes Granny to forget; not many thoughts remain.

She needs help all day long. It's how she makes it through. It's not my job, but I like to help and do what I can do.

I pray for Granny every night, for my family, and for a cure.

She doesn't remember me or my name, but she's still my granny **just the same.**

To you, the readers of all ages:

Thank you for reading this book about a very special subject. May you find joy in the life your loved one has lived and peace in the days to come. If your loved one is diagnosed with any form of dementia, they will need your help. Thank you for being there for them.

To my mother:

This book is dedicated to my beautiful mother, whom we affectionately call "Granny." You taught me how to love unconditionally. Alzheimer's tried to take away your mind and your thoughts, but it couldn't take your loving personality. The weeds could not take over your garden.

Meet the Author

Deborah L. Mills is a wife, mother, and grandmother. She enjoys writing and reading. She also likes to play with her grandchildren as often as possible. Deborah is caregiver for her mother who is diagnosed with Alzheimer's Disease.

This book was written with special help from **Jazéh** - my granddaughter, **Granny** – my mother, **Anastasia Korzh** – the best art director ever, and of course my husband and family.

Printed in the USA
CPSIA information can be obtained
at www.ICGtesting.com
LVHW061759210124
769531LV00006B/72